Pebble® Plus

Animal Kingdom Questions and Answers

Mammals
A Question and Answer Book

by Isabel Martin

Consulting Editor: Gail Saunders-Smith, PhD

CAPSTONE PRESS
a capstone imprint

Pebble Plus is published by Capstone Press,
1710 Roe Crest Drive, North Mankato, Minnesota 56003
www.capstonepub.com

Library of Congress Cataloging-in-Publication Data
Martin, Isabel, 1977– author.
  Mammals : a question and answer book / by Isabel Martin.
       pages cm. — (Pebble plus. Animal kingdom questions and answers)
Summary: "Simple text and colorful images illustrate types of mammals, including common characteristics, diet, and life cycle"—Provided by publisher.
  Audience: Ages 4–8.
  Audience: Grades K–3.
  Includes bibliographical references and index.
  ISBN 978-1-4914-0566-6 (library binding) — ISBN 978-1-4914-0634-2 (paperback) — ISBN 978-1-4914-0600-7 (eBook PDF)
  1. Mammals—Miscellanea—Juvenile literature. 2. Children's questions and answers. I. Title.
QL706.2M29 2015
599.02—dc23   2013050347

Editorial Credits
Nikki Bruno Clapper, editor; Cynthia Akiyoshi, designer; Kelly Garvin, media researcher;
Katy LaVigne, production specialist

Photo Credits
Dreamstime/Chris Lorenz, cover, back cover; FLPA/Imagebroker/Frank Sommariva, 17; Minden Pictures/D. Parer & E. Parer-Cook, 21; Shutterstock: AdStock RF, 11, Andreas Gradin, 9, CreativeNature.nl, 5, davemhuntphotography, 7, john michael evan potter, 13, Peter Schwarz, 19, worldswildlifewonders, 1, 15

Cover photo: mountain lion; title page photo: koalas

Note to Parents and Teachers

The Animal Kingdom Questions and Answers set supports national curriculum standards for science related to the diversity of living things. This book describes and illustrates the characteristics of mammals. The images support early readers in understanding the text. The repetition of words and phrases helps early readers learn new words. This book also introduces early readers to subject-specific vocabulary words, which are defined in the Glossary section. Early readers may need assistance to read some words and to use the Table of Contents, Glossary, Read More, Internet Sites, Critical Thinking Using the Common Core, and Index sections of the book.

Printed in the United States   5155

Table of Contents

Meet the Mammals

Scurry, scurry! A mouse races by.

Mice, bears, seals, elephants,

and wolves are all mammals.

People are mammals too!

yellow-necked mouse

Do Mammals Have Backbones?

Yes, mammals have backbones. A backbone is made up of small bones called vertebrae. The backbone is part of a mammal's skeleton.

Siberian tiger

Are Mammals Warm-Blooded or Cold-Blooded?

Mammals are warm-blooded.

Their body temperature stays the

same in hot and cold weather.

reindeer

What Type of Body Covering Do Mammals Have?

Mammals are covered with hair.

It helps keep them warm.

Most mammals have hair color

that blends in with their surroundings.

arctic fox

How Do Mammals Eat?

Mammals eat plants, meat, or both.
Teeth help them chew, bite, or tear
their food. Zebras eat grass.
Bats eat insects. Dolphins eat fish.

zebras

Where Do Mammals Live?

Mammals live on land or in water.

Sloths live in trees. Whales live in

the ocean. Camels live in deserts.

three-toed sloth

How Do Mammals Have Young?

Male and female mammals mate.

Babies grow inside their mothers.

Then mothers give birth to live young.

bison with calf

Do Mammals Care for Their Young?

Yes! Mammal babies drink milk

from their mothers.

Most mammal parents

stay with their babies and

teach them how to live.

lions

What Is a Cool Fact About Mammals?

The platypus is different from most mammals. It has a bill and webbed feet like a duck.

A platypus lays eggs. It does not give birth as other mammals do.

platypus

Glossary

bill—the hard front part of the mouth of birds, platypuses, and some dinosaurs

female—an animal that can give birth to young animals or lay eggs

mate—to join together to produce young

skeleton—the bones that support and protect the body of a human or other animal

sloth—a slow-moving animal that lives in the forests of South America

surroundings—the things around something or someone

temperature—the measure of how hot or cold something is

vertebra—one of the small bones that make up a backbone; vertebrae means more than one vertebra

warm-blooded—having a body temperature that stays about the same all the time

Read More

Berger, Melvin, and Gilda Berger. *Mammals*. Scholastic True or False. New York: Scholastic, 2011.

Jenkins, Martin. *Can We Save the Tiger?* Somerville, Mass.: Candlewick Press, 2011.

Stewart, Melissa. *Dolphins*. National Geographic Readers. Washington, D.C.: National Geographic, 2010.

Internet Sites

FactHound offers a safe, fun way to find Internet sites related to this book. All of the sites on FactHound have been researched by our staff.

Here's all you do:
Visit www.facthound.com
Type in this code: 9781491405666

Critical Thinking Using the Common Core

1. Where do three different kinds of mammals live? (Key Ideas and Details)

2. What would happen to the body temperature of a mammal if the animal's surroundings got colder? (Integration of Knowledge and Ideas)

Index

Word Count: 187
Grade: 1
Early-Intervention Level: 16